The
GREATEST
GIFT

The True Story of Christmas

Tyndale House Publishers, Inc.
WHEATON, ILLINOIS

CONTENTS

A Note to Readers

With 40 million copies in print, *The Living Bible* has been meeting a great need in people's hearts for more than thirty years. But even good things can be improved, so ninety evangelical scholars from various theological backgrounds and denominations were commissioned in 1989 to begin revising *The Living Bible*. The end result of this seven-year process is the *Holy Bible,* New Living Translation—a general-purpose translation that is accurate, easy to read, and excellent for study.

The goal of any Bible translation is to convey the meaning of the ancient Hebrew and Greek texts as accurately as possible to the modern reader. The New Living Translation is based on the most recent scholarship in the theory of translation. The challenge for the translators was to create a text that would make the same impact in the life of modern readers that the original text had for the original readers. In the New Living Translation, this is accomplished by translating entire thoughts (rather than just words) into natural, everyday English. The end result is a translation that is easy to read and understand and that accurately communicates the meaning of the original text.

We believe that this new translation, which combines the latest in scholarship with the best in translation style, will speak to your heart. We present the New Living Translation with the prayer that God will use it to speak his timeless truth to the church and to the world in a fresh, new way.

The Publishers
July 1996

The Greatest Gift

We have all watched children at Christmas, stars in their eyes, eagerly waiting to open gifts. Most of us share their anticipation and joy. Some gifts have been long needed, designed to fill a deep emotional void or real physical need. Some gifts have been long awaited, the fruit of hope or the fulfillment of a promise. The first Christmas gift, given long ago at the first Christmas, was given by God at great cost to answer our deepest needs and to fulfill God's most ancient promises.

Since the dawn of human history, we and all God's creation have suffered the damaging effects of human sin. When sin came into the world, it brought about our separation from God, from each other, and from the world God gave us. But God put into effect a plan for our restoration. He chose a man named Abraham to father a special nation. And through this nation of Israel and the family of King David came the solution to humankind's fall. The true story of Christmas records how God sent his Son to be born into King David's family, to live a human life, and to suffer a humiliating death on our behalf. God sent his Son as a gift—the greatest gift—a gift both long needed and long awaited.

The true story of Christmas is the agelong story of God's unstoppable love for the human race. It is the story of how God sent his Son, our Creator, to be born in a dirty stable, heralded by majestic angels, worshiped by humble shepherds, adored by dignified wise men. He is the fulfillment of God's promised plan for our forgiveness and restoration. By accepting the gift of Jesus, we can overcome the power of sin and be transformed by his presence in our life. We can let God rule in us today in anticipation of his near return, when he will rebuild his broken creation and reestablish his rule throughout the earth. What a glorious hope to celebrate this Christmas season!

THE GIFT PROMISED:
Hope in the Messiah

The Gift of Jesus the Messiah, though
in many ways surprising, did not
appear out of nowhere. He was the
fulfillment of a plan—God's plan—to
restore the perfection that had been
lost when people decided to disobey
God's instructions for life. God made
a good and beautiful world filled
with good and beautiful creatures.
But the people God put in this world
rejected the plan God had for them,
breaking their relationship with God.

But God, in his love, set out to re-establish his relationship with the lost human race. The Old Testament of the Bible records the story of how God chose Abraham and his descendants, the nation of Israel, to set the stage for the coming of his greatest gift—Jesus the Messiah—our hope. In the following Old Testament passages, watch as God's promised restoration unfolds.

Sin and Its Curse

GENESIS 3:14-19

This account in Genesis, the book of beginnings, records the consequences Adam and Eve suffered for disobeying God—consequences we still suffer today. Their disobedience led to our separation from God, the one who made us, and to our alienation from the rest of God's once-perfect creation. It led to intense pain in childbirth, to difficult toil in working the soil, and ultimately to death. But even as God leveled his curses against his broken creation, we are told that the woman's offspring would someday crush the serpent's head. This message foreshadows the promises made more explicit in later Scriptures of a Messiah or deliverer who would someday save us from the destructive power of sin. From the beginning of history, God promised a great gift—the birth of a child who would overcome sin and crush Satan, the deceiver.

So the LORD God said to the serpent, "Because you have done this, you will be punished. You are singled out from all the domestic and wild animals of the whole earth to be cursed. You will grovel in the dust as long as you live, crawling along on your belly. [15]From now on, you and the woman will be enemies, and your offspring and her offspring will be enemies. He will crush your head, and you will strike his heel."

¹⁶ Then he said to the woman, "You will bear children with intense pain and suffering. And though your desire will be for your husband,* he will be your master."

¹⁷ And to Adam he said, "Because you listened to your wife and ate the fruit I told you not to eat, I have placed a curse on the ground. All your life you will struggle to scratch a living from it. ¹⁸ It will grow thorns and thistles for you, though you will eat of its grains. ¹⁹ All your life you will sweat to produce food, until your dying day. Then you will return to the ground from which you came. For you were made from dust, and to the dust you will return."

3:16 Or *And though you may desire to control your husband.*

The Promise to Abraham

GENESIS 22:15-18

Though the book of Genesis records how a good world was broken by sin, it doesn't leave us in despair. It tells us how God chose an obedient man named Abraham to father a special nation through whom the entire world would be blessed. God gave Abraham a son named Isaac, who was born to him and Sarah in their old age. It was through Isaac that Abraham expected God's promises of blessing to be fulfilled. But when God asked Abraham to offer his son back to him, God returned his son with this amazing promise. God would give Abraham many descendants through whom the entire world would be blessed. This promise was ultimately fulfilled in the gift of Jesus the Messiah, who was among Abraham's descendants.

Then the angel of the LORD called again to Abraham from heaven, [16] "This is what the LORD says: Because you have obeyed me and have not withheld even your beloved son, I swear by my own self that [17] I will bless you richly. I will multiply your descendants into countless millions, like the stars of the sky and the sand on the seashore. They will conquer their enemies, [18] and through your descendants,* all the nations of the earth will be blessed—all because you have obeyed me."

The Promise to David

2 SAMUEL 7:8-16
One of Abraham's descendants was David, and God continued his promise of blessing and restoration through David's family. God promised that David's royal line would carry on forever, a promise eventually realized in
22:18 Hebrew *seed.*

*the birth of Jesus the Messiah. David's
earthly dynasty of kings ended four
centuries after his reign, but Jesus,
one of David's direct descendants,
was the ultimate fulfillment of that
promise (Luke 1:30-33; Acts 2:22-
36). Jesus will reign for eternity—
already in his spiritual kingdom and,
after his return, in the new Jerusalem
(Revelation 21).*

"Now go [Nathan] and say to my servant David, 'This is what the LORD
Almighty says: I chose you to lead my
people Israel when you were just a
shepherd boy, tending your sheep out
in the pasture. 9I have been with you
wherever you have gone, and I have
destroyed all your enemies. Now I
will make your name famous throughout the earth! 10And I have provided a
permanent homeland for my people
Israel, a secure place where they will

never be disturbed. It will be their own land where wicked nations won't oppress them as they did in the past, [11]from the time I appointed judges to rule my people. And I will keep you safe from all your enemies.

"'And now the LORD declares that he will build a house for you—a dynasty of kings! [12]For when you die, I will raise up one of your descendants, and I will make his kingdom strong. [13]He is the one who will build a house— a temple—for my name. And I will establish the throne of his kingdom forever. [14]I will be his father, and he will be my son. If he sins, I will use other nations to punish him. [15]But my unfailing love will not be taken from him as I took it from Saul, whom I removed before you. [16]Your dynasty and your kingdom will continue for all time before me, and your throne will be secure forever.'"

Immanuel—God Is with Us!

ISAIAH 7:10-16

The prophet Isaiah spoke this message to Ahaz, one of King David's descendants, centuries before the birth of Jesus. Matthew, the Gospel writer, quoted Isaiah 7:14 to show that this prophecy was fulfilled through the virgin Mary (Matthew 1:23), who had a son named Jesus. This child was truly Immanuel, meaning, "God is with us." When Jesus Christ was born, God came to live among people as a human, present with us as never before.

Not long after this, the LORD sent this message to King Ahaz: ¹¹"Ask me for a sign, Ahaz, to prove that I will crush your enemies as I have promised. Ask for anything you like, and make it as difficult as you want."

¹²But the king refused. "No," he

said, "I wouldn't test the LORD like that."

¹³Then Isaiah said, "Listen well, you royal family of David! You aren't satisfied to exhaust my patience. You exhaust the patience of God as well! ¹⁴All right then, the Lord himself will choose the sign. Look! The virgin* will conceive a child! She will give birth to a son and will call him Immanuel— 'God is with us.' ¹⁵By the time this child is old enough to eat curds and honey, he will know enough to choose what is right and reject what is wrong. ¹⁶But before he knows right from wrong, the two kings you fear so much—the kings of Israel and Aram—will both be dead.

Hope in the Coming Messiah
ISAIAH 9:1-2, 6-7
The prophet Isaiah spoke of a child who would become Israel's deliverer and

7:14 Or *young woman.*

ruler (9:6). *Matthew quoted these verses in describing the ministry of Jesus (Matthew 4:15-16). The territories of Zebulun and Naphtali represented the northern kingdom but were also the territories around Galilee where Jesus grew up and often ministered. That is why the people would see "a great light." In a time of great darkness, God sent a light who shined on everyone living in the shadow of death. He is both " Wonderful Counselor" and "Mighty God," born to establish his eternal Kingdom and to deliver all people from their slavery to sin.*

Nevertheless, that time of darkness and despair will not go on forever. The land of Zebulun and Naphtali will soon be humbled, but there will be a time in the future when Galilee of the Gentiles, which lies along the road that runs between the Jordan and the sea, will be filled with glory. ²The people who walk in darkness will see a great light— a light that will shine on all who live in the land where death casts its shadow.

*   *   *

⁶For a child is born to us, a son is given to us. And the government will rest on his shoulders. These will be his royal titles: Wonderful Counselor,* Mighty God, Everlasting Father, Prince of Peace. ⁷His ever expanding, peaceful government will never end. He will rule forever with fairness and justice from the throne of his ancestor David. The passionate commitment of the LORD Almighty will guarantee this!

A Ruler from Bethlehem
MICAH 5:2-5a
Centuries before Jesus' birth, the prophet Micah predicted the coming of an eternal ruler, "whose origins are
9:6 Or *Wonderful, Counselor.*

12

from the distant past." The prophet also predicted that Bethlehem would be the birthplace of this ruler. This promised eternal King, a descendant of King David, did come to live as a man. Although he was eternal, Jesus Christ entered human history as a baby born in the town of Bethlehem. And though he died on a Roman cross, he rose from the dead to his present heavenly reign, and he will rule throughout eternity.

But you, O Bethlehem Ephrathah, are only a small village in Judah. Yet a ruler of Israel will come from you, one whose origins are from the distant past. [3]The people of Israel will be abandoned to their enemies until the time when the woman in labor gives birth to her son. Then at last his fellow countrymen will return from exile to their own land. [4]And he will stand to lead his flock with the LORD's strength, in the majesty of the name of the LORD his God. Then his people will live there undisturbed, for he will be highly honored all around the world. ⁵And he will be the source of our peace.

The Suffering Servant
ISAIAH 53:1-12

This chapter from Isaiah expands on the promises of the Messiah, who would suffer for the sins of all people. Such a prophecy, given long before Jesus' birth, is astounding! Who would have believed that God would choose to save the world through a humble, suffering servant rather than a glorious king? The idea is contrary to human pride and worldly ways. But God often works in ways we don't expect. It was revealed in this passage that the Messiah's strength would be shown in humility, and Jesus Christ lived this out to perfection.

Who has believed our message? To whom will the LORD reveal his saving power? ²My servant grew up in the LORD's presence like a tender green shoot, sprouting from a root in dry and sterile ground. There was nothing beautiful or majestic about his appearance, nothing to attract us to him. ³He was despised and rejected—a man of sorrows, acquainted with bitterest grief. We turned our backs on him and looked the other way when he went by. He was despised, and we did not care.

⁴Yet it was our weaknesses he carried; it was our sorrows* that weighed him down. And we thought his troubles were a punishment from God for his own sins! ⁵But he was wounded and crushed for our sins. He was beaten

53:4 Or *Yet it was our sicknesses he carried; it was our diseases.*

that we might have peace. He was whipped, and we were healed! ⁶All of us have strayed away like sheep. We have left God's paths to follow our own. Yet the LORD laid on him the guilt and sins of us all.

⁷He was oppressed and treated harshly, yet he never said a word. He was led as a lamb to the slaughter. And as a sheep is silent before the shearers, he did not open his mouth. ⁸From prison and trial they led him away to his death. But who among the people realized that he was dying for their sins—that he was suffering their punishment? ⁹He had done no wrong, and he never deceived anyone. But he was buried like a criminal; he was put in a rich man's grave.

¹⁰But it was the LORD's good plan to crush him and fill him with grief. Yet when his life is made an offering for sin, he will have a multitude of chil-

dren, many heirs. He will enjoy a long life, and the LORD's plan will prosper in his hands. ¹¹When he sees all that is accomplished by his anguish, he will be satisfied. And because of what he has experienced, my righteous servant will make it possible for many to be counted righteous, for he will bear all their sins. ¹²I will give him the honors of one who is mighty and great, because he exposed himself to death. He was counted among those who were sinners. He bore the sins of many and interceded for sinners.

Good News for the Oppressed

ISAIAH 61:1-9
Long after the prophet Isaiah recorded this message, Jesus read it to demonstrate that he was the promised Messiah. After reading the first two verses, Jesus stopped and said, "This Scripture has come true today before your very eyes!"

(Luke 4:21). The people had witnessed Jesus' ministry to the poor and oppressed, a ministry that had been predicted centuries earlier! Through his acts of mercy, Jesus was demonstrating his power over sin and its painful consequences. These were blessings of God's Kingdom and the promised Messiah's rule, blessings that we can partake of today by making Jesus the Lord of our life.

The Spirit of the Sovereign LORD is upon me, because the LORD has appointed me to bring good news to the poor. He has sent me to comfort the brokenhearted and to announce that captives will be released and prisoners will be freed. * ²He has sent me to tell those who mourn that the time of the LORD's favor has come,* and with it, the day of God's anger against their enemies. ³To all who mourn in

61:1 Greek version reads *and the blind will see.* 61:2 Or *to proclaim the acceptable year of the LORD*

Israel, * he will give beauty for ashes, joy instead of mourning, praise instead of despair. For the LORD has planted them like strong and graceful oaks for his own glory.

⁴They will rebuild the ancient ruins, repairing cities long ago destroyed. They will revive them, though they have been empty for many generations. ⁵Foreigners will be your servants. They will feed your flocks and plow your fields and tend your vineyards. ⁶You will be called priests of the LORD, ministers of our God. You will be fed with the treasures of the nations and will boast in their riches. ⁷Instead of shame and dishonor, you will inherit a double portion of prosperity and everlasting joy.

⁸"For I, the LORD, love justice. I hate robbery and wrongdoing. I will faithfully reward my people for their

61:3 Hebrew *in Zion.*

61:3 Hebrew *in Zion.*

suffering and make an everlasting covenant with them. ⁹Their descendants will be known and honored among the nations. Everyone will realize that they are a people the LORD has blessed."

THE GIFT GIVEN:
The True Story of Christmas

God's special gift of Jesus came to us in a surprising way. We probably would have expected the Creator of the universe to come in a blaze of glory, or at least to be born into a family of wealth and influence. But Jesus was born to a peasant girl in a dirty Bethlehem stable. And she was engaged to a humble carpenter from the town of Nazareth in Galilee. Both were distant descendants of King David. The first visitors of Jesus were simple shepherds, who had heard the angels' announcement while watching their sheep. The child was also visited by wisemen from eastern lands, who, though wealthy, were foreigners and would not have been expected to watch for the fulfillment of God's promises to Israel. In the story of Christmas, this truth rings crystal clear: Jesus came for everyone. God's gift of Jesus is for poor and wealthy alike; it is for people of all races and social backgrounds. The gift God gave that first Christmas is for us all.

An Angel Speaks to Mary
LUKE 1:26-38

In the sixth month of Elizabeth's pregnancy, God sent the angel Gabriel to Nazareth, a village in Galilee, [27] to a virgin named Mary. She was engaged to be married to a man named

Joseph, a descendant of King David.
28Gabriel appeared to her and said,
"Greetings, favored woman! The Lord
is with you!*"

29Confused and disturbed, Mary
tried to think what the angel could
mean. 30"Don't be frightened, Mary,"
the angel told her, "for God has
decided to bless you! 31You will
become pregnant and have a son, and
you are to name him Jesus. 32He will
be very great and will be called the
Son of the Most High. And the Lord
God will give him the throne of his
ancestor David. 33And he will reign
over Israel* forever; his Kingdom will
never end!"

34Mary asked the angel, "But how
can I have a baby? I am a virgin."

35The angel replied, "The Holy Spirit
will come upon you, and the power of
the Most High will overshadow you. So

1:28 Some manuscripts add *Blessed are you among women.*
1:33 Greek *over the house of Jacob.*

the baby born to you will be holy, and he will be called the Son of God. ³⁶ What's more, your relative Elizabeth has become pregnant in her old age! People used to say she was barren, but she's already in her sixth month. ³⁷For nothing is impossible with God."

³⁸Mary responded, "I am the Lord's servant, and I am willing to accept whatever he wants. May everything you have said come true." And then the angel left.

Mary's Song of Praise
LUKE 1:39-56

A few days later Mary hurried to the hill country of Judea, to the town ⁴⁰where Zechariah lived. She entered the house and greeted Elizabeth. ⁴¹At the sound of Mary's greeting, Elizabeth's child leaped within her, and Elizabeth was filled with the Holy Spirit.

⁴²Elizabeth gave a glad cry and

exclaimed to Mary, "You are blessed by God above all other women, and your child is blessed. ⁴³ What an honor this is, that the mother of my Lord should visit me! ⁴⁴ When you came in and greeted me, my baby jumped for joy the instant I heard your voice! ⁴⁵ You are blessed, because you believed that the Lord would do what he said."

⁴⁶Mary responded,

"Oh, how I praise the Lord.
⁴⁷   How I rejoice in God my Savior!
⁴⁸ For he took notice of his lowly
        servant girl,
     and now generation after
        generation
        will call me blessed.
⁴⁹ For he, the Mighty One, is holy,
     and he has done great things for
        me.
⁵⁰ His mercy goes on from generation
        to generation,
     to all who fear him.

⁵¹ His mighty arm does tremendous
    things!
  How he scatters the proud and
    haughty ones!
⁵² He has taken princes from their
    thrones
  and exalted the lowly.

⁵³ He has satisfied the hungry with
    good things
  and sent the rich away with
    empty hands.
⁵⁴ And how he has helped his servant
    Israel!
  He has not forgotten his promise
    to be merciful.
⁵⁵ For he promised our
    ancestors—Abraham and his
    children—
  to be merciful to them forever."

⁵⁶Mary stayed with Elizabeth about
three months and then went back to
her own home.

An Angel's Message to Joseph

MATTHEW 1:18-25

Now this is how Jesus the Messiah was born. His mother, Mary, was engaged to be married to Joseph. But while she was still a virgin, she became pregnant by the Holy Spirit. [19]Joseph, her fiancé, being a just man, decided to break the engagement quietly, so as not to disgrace her publicly.

[20]As he considered this, he fell asleep, and an angel of the Lord appeared to him in a dream. "Joseph, son of David," the angel said, "do not be afraid to go ahead with your marriage to Mary. For the child within her has been conceived by the Holy Spirit. [21]And she will have a son, and you are to name him Jesus,* for he will save his people from their sins." [22]All of this happened to fulfill the Lord's message through his prophet:

1:21 *Jesus* means "The LORD saves."

23 "Look! The virgin will conceive a
      child!
   She will give birth to a son,
  and he will be called Immanuel*
   (meaning, God is with us)."

24 When Joseph woke up, he did what
the angel of the Lord commanded.
He brought Mary home to be his wife,
25but she remained a virgin until her
son was born. And Joseph named
him Jesus.

The Birth of Jesus

LUKE 2:1-20

At that time the Roman emperor,
Augustus, decreed that a census should
be taken throughout the Roman Empire.
2(This was the first census taken when
Quirinius was governor of Syria.) 3All
returned to their own towns to register
for this census. 4And because Joseph

1:23 Isa 7:14; 8:8, 10.

was a descendant of King David, he had to go to Bethlehem in Judea, David's ancient home. He traveled there from the village of Nazareth in Galilee. ⁵He took with him Mary, his fiancée, who was obviously pregnant by this time.

⁶And while they were there, the time came for her baby to be born. ⁷She gave birth to her first child, a son. She wrapped him snugly in strips of cloth and laid him in a manger, because there was no room for them in the village inn.

⁸That night some shepherds were in the fields outside the village, guarding their flocks of sheep. ⁹Suddenly, an angel of the Lord appeared among them, and the radiance of the Lord's glory surrounded them. They were terribly frightened, ¹⁰but the angel reassured them. "Don't be afraid!" he said. "I bring you good news of great joy for

everyone! ¹¹ The Savior—yes, the Messiah, the Lord—has been born tonight in Bethlehem, the city of David! ¹²And this is how you will recognize him: You will find a baby lying in a manger, wrapped snugly in strips of cloth!"

¹³Suddenly, the angel was joined by a vast host of others—the armies of heaven—praising God:

¹⁴ "Glory to God in the highest heaven,
    and peace on earth to all whom
        God favors. *"

¹⁵When the angels had returned to heaven, the shepherds said to each other, "Come on, let's go to Bethlehem! Let's see this wonderful thing that has happened, which the Lord has told us about."

¹⁶They ran to the village and found Mary and Joseph. And there was the baby, lying in the manger. ¹⁷Then the

2:14 Or *and peace on earth for all those pleasing God;* some manuscripts read *and peace on earth, goodwill among people.*

shepherds told everyone what had happened and what the angel had said to them about this child. ¹⁸All who heard the shepherds' story were astonished, ¹⁹but Mary quietly treasured these things in her heart and thought about them often. ²⁰The shepherds went back to their fields and flocks, glorifying and praising God for what the angels had told them, and because they had seen the child, just as the angel had said.

The Visit of the Wise Men
MATTHEW 2:1-23

Jesus was born in the town of Bethlehem in Judea, during the reign of King Herod. About that time some wise men* from eastern lands arrived in Jerusalem, asking, ²"Where is the newborn king of the Jews? We have seen his star as it arose,* and we have come to worship him."

2:1 Or *royal astrologers;* Greek reads *magi;* also in 2:7, 16.
2:2 Or *in the east.*

³Herod was deeply disturbed by their question, as was all of Jerusalem. ⁴He called a meeting of the leading priests and teachers of religious law. "Where did the prophets say the Messiah would be born?" he asked them.

⁵"In Bethlehem," they said, "for this is what the prophet wrote:

⁶ 'O Bethlehem of Judah,
    you are not just a lowly village
        in Judah,
for a ruler will come from you
    who will be the shepherd for my
        people Israel.'"*

⁷Then Herod sent a private message to the wise men, asking them to come see him. At this meeting he learned the exact time when they first saw the star. ⁸Then he told them, "Go to Bethlehem and search carefully for the

2:6 Mic 5:2; 2 Sam 5:2.

child. And when you find him, come back and tell me so that I can go and worship him, too!"

⁹After this interview the wise men went their way. Once again the star appeared to them, guiding them to Bethlehem. It went ahead of them and stopped over the place where the child was. ¹⁰When they saw the star, they were filled with joy! ¹¹They entered the house where the child and his mother, Mary, were, and they fell down before him and worshiped him. Then they opened their treasure chests and gave him gifts of gold, frankincense, and myrrh. ¹²But when it was time to leave, they went home another way, because God had warned them in a dream not to return to Herod.

¹³After the wise men were gone, an angel of the Lord appeared to Joseph in a dream. "Get up and flee to Egypt

with the child and his mother," the angel said. "Stay there until I tell you to return, because Herod is going to try to kill the child." ¹⁴That night Joseph left for Egypt with the child and Mary, his mother, ¹⁵and they stayed there until Herod's death. This fulfilled what the Lord had spoken through the prophet: "I called my Son out of Egypt."*

¹⁶Herod was furious when he learned that the wise men had outwitted him. He sent soldiers to kill all the boys in and around Bethlehem who were two years old and under, because the wise men had told him the star first appeared to them about two years earlier.* ¹⁷Herod's brutal action fulfilled the prophecy of Jeremiah:

¹⁸ "A cry of anguish is heard in Ramah—
weeping and mourning unrestrained.

2:15 Hos 11:1.   2:16 Or *according to the time he calculated from the wise men.*

Rachel weeps for her children,
refusing to be comforted—for
they are dead."*

¹⁹When Herod died, an angel of
the Lord appeared in a dream to
Joseph in Egypt and told him, ²⁰"Get
up and take the child and his mother
back to the land of Israel, because
those who were trying to kill the
child are dead." ²¹So Joseph returned
immediately to Israel with Jesus and
his mother. ²²But when he learned
that the new ruler was Herod's son
Archelaus, he was afraid. Then, in
another dream, he was warned to go
to Galilee. ²³So they went and lived
in a town called Nazareth. This fulfilled what was spoken by the prophets
concerning the Messiah: "He will be
called a Nazarene."

2:18 Jer 31:15.

THE GIFT RECEIVED:
New Life in Christ

God wanted to renew his relationship with his sinful, broken creation.
When the right time came, he sent
the gift of a Savior. Jesus came to
fulfill God's plan. God wants us to
be his children and to live the abun-
dant life he always intended. He
wants to live in us and transform us
to be like his Son, Jesus, reversing
the damaging power of sin that has
infected the lives of all people ever
since Adam and Eve first chose to

disobey. The New Testament teaches us what it means to live the new life we can have because Jesus was born as a human baby, lived his self-giving life, and died to pay the debt of our sin. In the following passages, discover how the gift of Jesus has changed everything. Discover what it means to receive this special gift of restoration and forgiveness— new life in Jesus Christ.

Christ, the Eternal Word

JOHN 1:1-14

What Jesus taught and what he did are tied inseparably to who he is. John shows that Jesus was both fully human and fully God. Although Jesus took upon himself full humanity and lived as a man, he never ceased to be the eternal God who has always existed. He is the Creator and Sustainer of all things and the source of eternal life.

It is this truth that makes him the perfect gift to broken humanity. As God, he could offer us forgiveness; as a man, he could suffer on our behalf, paying our debt of sin. If we cannot or do not believe this basic truth, we will not be able to receive God's gift of eternal life, which is ours through Jesus Christ.

In the beginning the Word already existed. He was with God, and he was God. ²He was in the beginning with God. ³He created everything there is. Nothing exists that he didn't make. ⁴Life itself was in him, and this life gives light to everyone. ⁵ The light shines through the darkness, and the darkness can never extinguish it.

⁶God sent John the Baptist ⁷to tell everyone about the light so that everyone might believe because of

1:14 Greek *grace and truth;* also in 1:17.

his testimony. ⁸John himself was not the light; he was only a witness to the light. ⁹The one who is the true light, who gives light to everyone, was going to come into the world.

¹⁰But although the world was made through him, the world didn't recognize him when he came. ¹¹Even in his own land and among his own people, he was not accepted. ¹²But to all who believed him and accepted him, he gave the right to become children of God. ¹³They are reborn! This is not a physical birth resulting from human passion or plan—this rebirth comes from God.

¹⁴So the Word became human and lived here on earth among us. He was full of unfailing love and faithfulness.* And we have seen his glory, the glory of the only Son of the Father.

Born Again through Faith

JOHN 3:1-17

The message of the entire Bible comes to a focus as Jesus speaks to Nicodemus. God sent his Son to become a part of his sin-broken creation, so that he would overcome sin and death and restore our relationship with God. In John 3:16 we are told that God gave the special gift of his Son for a specific and wonderful purpose. Through belief in Jesus we can have eternal life; the power of sin and death has been overcome by his death on the cross. The gift of Jesus at Christmas has fulfilled God's ancient promises of restoration. He paid dearly with the life of his Son, the highest price he could pay. Jesus accepted our punishment, paid the price for our sins, and now he offers us the new life he purchased.

After dark one evening, a Jewish religious leader named Nicodemus, a

Pharisee, [2]came to speak with Jesus. "Teacher," he said, "we all know that God has sent you to teach us. Your miraculous signs are proof enough that God is with you."

[3]Jesus replied, "I assure you, unless you are born again,* you can never see the Kingdom of God."

[4]"What do you mean?" exclaimed Nicodemus. "How can an old man go back into his mother's womb and be born again?"

[5]Jesus replied, "The truth is, no one can enter the Kingdom of God without being born of water and the Spirit. * [6]Humans can reproduce only human life, but the Holy Spirit gives new life from heaven. [7]So don't be surprised at my statement that you* must be born again. [8]Just as you can hear the wind but can't tell where it

3:3 Or *born from above*; also in 3:7. 3:5 Or *spirit.* The Greek word for *Spirit* can also be translated *wind*; see 3:8. 3:7 The Greek word for *you* is plural; also in 3:12

comes from or where it is going, so you can't explain how people are born of the Spirit."

⁹"What do you mean?" Nicodemus asked.

¹⁰Jesus replied, "You are a respected Jewish teacher, and yet you don't understand these things? ¹¹I assure you, I am telling you what we know and have seen, and yet you won't believe us. ¹²But if you don't even believe me when I tell you about things that happen here on earth, how can you possibly believe if I tell you what is going on in heaven? ¹³For only I, the Son of Man,* have come to earth and will return to heaven again. ¹⁴And as Moses lifted up the bronze snake on a pole in the wilderness, so I, the Son of Man, must be lifted up on a pole,* ¹⁵so that everyone who believes in me will have eternal life.

3:13 Some manuscripts add *who lives in heaven.*   3:14 Greek *must be lifted up*

¹⁶"For God so loved the world that he gave his only Son, so that everyone who believes in him will not perish but have eternal life. ¹⁷God did not send his Son into the world to condemn it, but to save it."

Sin's Power Is Broken

ROMANS 6:1-14

Since the first sin of Adam and Eve in the Garden of Eden, the human race has yearned for a solution to the sin problem. God sent his Son to be born as a baby to make new life possible. We can enjoy it because we are united with Jesus Christ in his death and resurrection. Our evil desires, our bondage to sin, and our love of sin died with him. Now, united by faith in him and in his resurrection life, we have unbroken fellowship with God and freedom from sin's hold on us.

Well then, should we keep on sinning so that God can show us more and more kindness and forgiveness? [2]Of course not! Since we have died to sin, how can we continue to live in it? [3]Or have you forgotten that when we became Christians and were baptized to become one with Christ Jesus, we died with him? [4]For we died and were buried with Christ by baptism. And just as Christ was raised from the dead by the glorious power of the Father, now we also may live new lives.

[5]Since we have been united with him in his death, we will also be raised as he was. [6]Our old sinful selves were crucified with Christ so that sin might lose its power in our lives. We are no longer slaves to sin. [7]For when we died with Christ we were set free from the power of sin. [8]And since we died with Christ, we know we will also share his new life.

⁹We are sure of this because Christ rose from the dead, and he will never die again. Death no longer has any power over him. ¹⁰He died once to defeat sin, and now he lives for the glory of God. ¹¹So you should consider yourselves dead to sin and able to live for the glory of God through Christ Jesus.

¹²Do not let sin control the way you live;* do not give in to its lustful desires. ¹³Do not let any part of your body become a tool of wickedness, to be used for sinning. Instead, give yourselves completely to God since you have been given new life. And use your whole body as a tool to do what is right for the glory of God. ¹⁴Sin is no longer your master, for you are no longer subject to the law, which enslaves you to sin. Instead, you are free by God's grace.

6:12 Or *Do not let sin reign in your body, which is subject to death.*

Living the New Life

Because of the gift of Jesus, we have been given a new life. We can put on a brand-new nature by accepting Jesus Christ and regarding our earthly nature as dead. We change our behavior by letting Christ live within us, so that he can shape us into what we should be. Sin no longer rules our life as we put heaven's priorities into daily practice. As we allow God to change us, we are taking part in his transforming work in the world. Through Jesus Christ, God is now in the process of reversing the effects of sin on his creation. And when Jesus returns, he will complete this work of re-creation in our broken world.

Since you have been raised to new life with Christ, set your sights on the realities of heaven, where Christ sits at God's right hand in the place of honor

3:4 Some manuscripts read *our.*

and power. ²Let heaven fill your thoughts. Do not think only about things down here on earth. ³For you died when Christ died, and your real life is hidden with Christ in God. ⁴And when Christ, who is your* real life, is revealed to the whole world, you will share in all his glory.

⁵So put to death the sinful, earthly things lurking within you. Have nothing to do with sexual sin, impurity, lust, and shameful desires. Don't be greedy for the good things of this life, for that is idolatry. ⁶God's terrible anger will come upon those who do such things. ⁷You used to do them when your life was still part of this world. ⁸But now is the time to get rid of anger, rage, malicious behavior, slander, and dirty language. ⁹Don't lie to each other, for you have stripped off your old evil nature and all its wicked deeds. ¹⁰In its place you

have clothed yourselves with a brand-new nature that is continually being renewed as you learn more and more about Christ, who created this new nature within you. ¹¹In this new life, it doesn't matter if you are a Jew or a Gentile,* circumcised or uncircumcised, barbaric, uncivilized,* slave, or free. Christ is all that matters, and he lives in all of us.

¹²Since God chose you to be the holy people whom he loves, you must clothe yourselves with tenderhearted mercy, kindness, humility, gentleness, and patience. ¹³You must make allowance for each other's faults and forgive the person who offends you. Remember, the Lord forgave you, so you must forgive others. ¹⁴And the most important piece of clothing you must wear is love. Love is what binds us all together in perfect harmony. ¹⁵And let the peace

3:11a Greek *Greek*.   3:11b Greek *Barbarian, Scythian*.

that comes from Christ rule in your
hearts. For as members of one body
you are all called to live in peace. And
always be thankful.

HOW YOU CAN
KNOW GOD

Purpose, meaning, a reason for living—these are all things we desire and search for in life. But despite our search, we still feel empty and unfulfilled. We each have an empty place in our heart, a spiritual void, a "God-shaped vacuum." Possessions won't fill it, nor will success, relationships, or even religion. Only through a vibrant relationship with God can this void be filled. But before such a relationship can be established, we need to face a serious problem.

The Problem: Sin

The Bible identifies this problem as sin. Sin is not just the bad things we do but an inherent part of who we are. We are not sinners because we sin; we sin because we are sinners. King David once wrote, "I was born a sinner—yes, from the moment my mother conceived me" (Psalm 51:5). Because we are born sinners, sinning comes to us naturally. Scripture tells us, " The human heart is most deceitful and desperately wicked. Who really knows how bad it is? " (Jeremiah 17:9). Every problem we experience in society today can be traced back to our refusal to live God's way.

The Solution: Jesus Christ

God understood our problem and knew we could not solve it alone. So he lovingly sent his own Son, Jesus Christ, to bridge the chasm of sin that separates us from God. Jesus laid

aside his divine privileges and walked
the earth as a man, experiencing all
the troubles and emotions that we do.
He was arrested on false charges and
killed on a Roman cross. But this was
no accident. He willingly suffered the
punishment deserved by us all. And
then three days later, Jesus rose from
the dead, conquering sin and death
forever!

The Response:
Accepting God's Offer

To know Jesus Christ personally and
have our sins forgiven, we must ac-
knowledge that we are sinners sepa-
rated from God and that our only hope
is Jesus Christ, the Son of God, who
came and died for our sins. But we
must not stop with this realization. We
also need to confess and turn from our
sins. And then we must invite Jesus
Christ into our life as Lord and Savior.

He will move in and help us to change from the inside out.

If you are ready to repent of your sins and accept Jesus Christ as your personal Savior so that you can receive his forgiveness, take a moment to pray:

> God, I'm sorry for my sins. Right now, I turn from my sins and ask you to forgive me. Thank you for sending Jesus Christ to die on the cross for my sins. Jesus, I ask you to come into my life and be my Lord, Savior, and Friend. Thank you for forgiving me and giving me eternal life. In Jesus' name I pray, amen.

If you prayed this prayer and meant it, you can be sure that God has forgiven you and received you into his family.

The New Living Translation is available in a wide variety of popular Bible editions, including

DELUXE TEXT EDITION
The *Holy Bible,* Deluxe Text Edition, is perfect for anyone who wishes to experience God's Word through the New Living Translation.

LIFE APPLICATION® STUDY BIBLE
This best-selling study Bible contains over 10,000 Life Application notes to help you apply the truth of God's Word to everyday life.

TOUCHPOINT® BIBLE
The *TouchPoint Bible* quickly directs you to specific passages in God's Word on hundreds of topics you are likely to face.

THE ONE YEAR® BIBLE
The One Year Bible is unique; no other read-through-the-Bible plan offers the convenience found here.

THE BOOK
The Book is a nonthreatening, easy-to-read, contemporary Bible for those new to the Scriptures. Includes book introductions and other helps on how the Bible relates to life.

STUDENT'S LIFE APPLICATION® BIBLE
This popular teen study Bible will help today's young people easily discover God's perspective and how to apply it to their lives.

SLIMLINE REFERENCE BIBLE
You can enjoy the New Living Translation in a special slimline edition. The Slimline Reference Bible offers a variety of features in an ultrathin design.

THE ROCK
The Rock helps guide teenagers' daily decision making as they wrestle with tough moral dilemmas. Includes hundreds of notes and features for building a strong moral foundation.